NEW · WORKS · FOR
MECCANO · LIMITED
LIVERPOOL

FRANK HORNBY

The Boy Who Made
$1,000,000
With A Toy

By

M. P. GOULD

Fredonia Books
Amsterdam, The Netherlands

Frank Hornby:
The Boy Who Made $1,000,000 with a Toy

by
M. P. Gould

ISBN: 1-4101-0792-2

Fredonia Books
Amsterdam, The Netherlands
http://www.fredoniabooks.com

CONTENTS

PREFACE.

"START SOMETHING."

"Start Something" has two meanings. When you tease your little sister, pester your pals, try to fool your father or trick your teacher, you are "starting something."

And when you play with blocks, lay tracks and run trains, and then set up a wireless outfit or build derricks, steamboats, automobiles, and bridges; or still later make money by thinking up some special scheme and putting it through— you are "starting something" of a different character.

Every boy has a natural desire to "start something." He wants to build, or make, or invent new things, or new and better ways of doing old things.

"*Penrod*," in Booth Tarkington's book, was an inventor; he was always "starting something," but always getting into trouble, playing pranks, getting ahead of the other boys, deceiving his parents. Some people think *"Penrod"* is almost as bad as *"Nick Carter,"* or *"Huckleberry Finn."*

Frank Hornby "started something" a long time ago and now he is a millionaire. He "started" because he read a book called *"Self Help"* which was written by Samuel Smiles, and which tells the stories of great men who have invented useful things, and of how they, too, "started something" and stuck to it until success crowned their efforts.

Frank Hornby invented a toy that is making it easy for boys all over the world to start building aeroplanes; constructing bridges; designing automobiles and a thousand other things. By playing with this invention any boy can learn how to make many things that are practical and useful, and may "start something" that will help make money for him when he grows up.

I have written the story of how Frank Hornby "started something" so that boys all over America might know how he succeeded, and might find in his experience, ideas which would enable them to "start something" and perhaps make a million dollars also.

Few of us like to read books that are dull and dry. We like books that are exciting and that rouse our ambitions and make us long to be like the people we read about. *"Treasure Island"* makes us want to be a pirate. *"Ivanhoe"* makes us want to be a brave, fearless Knight and rescue fair maidens from castle dungeons. *"The Last of the Mohicans"* makes us want to be crafty in the woods and escape from the "Murderous Indians." *"Arabian Nights"* fills us with a feeling of mystery and awe, while *"Robinson Crusoe"* stirs up our imagination and makes us want to be left alone on a desolate island, and do the

9

things he did. *"Rab and His Friends"* makes us love dogs, while no one can read *"Black Beauty"* without wanting to own and pet, and ride and drive, a pony just like *"Black Beauty."*

"Wild Animals I Have Known" makes us feel as if we actually knew the wily wolf, the sly fox, the sleepy old bear and all the other animals.

None of us like to have people "preach" to us; it makes us uncomfortable; it sounds too much like scolding. We like to read fascinating books; we like to learn things, too, but in a pleasant way. We like to become really interested in reading, because then we learn so much easier—and have a lot of fun at the same time.

And so it has been my aim to tell the story of Frank Hornby and his fight for success in an interesting style; and to tell as well, things that will help boys succeed; that will show them the principles on which all success is built.

If this story inspires you to "start

something" worth while and carry it on
to success, and perhaps make a lot of
money and become a strong, successful
man—if it makes you want to do what
Frank Hornby did—then I will consider
this the best book I have ever written.

M. P. GOULD.

CHAPTER I.

WHAT STARTED
FRANK HORNBY TO THINKING.

Frank Hornby was an English boy. He was born in Liverpool in 1863 while Abraham Lincoln was President of the United States and Queen Victoria was the ruler of Great Britain. His father was a Liverpool provision merchant. He bought and sold all kinds of produce.

Mrs. Hornby, Frank's mother, was a most unusual Christian woman. She was a dreamer, a lover of music. Her life was filled with romance. Like all good mothers she dreamed great achievements for her boy and for his sister.

Frank's sister has also developed into a very remarkable character. She is a fearless and famous missionary in China. She has faced death many times. She

13

went through the Boxer Revolution. She is not afraid to go anywhere and every where in China. She speaks Chinese fluently and seems to bear a charmed life. Being a doctor, she has been able to do wonderful things for the sick and has become very much beloved in China —but that is another story.

A great many English boys go to private school, but Mr. Hornby was an American in his democracy. He believed in public schools and so Frank went to a public school until he was sixteen years of age. Then he entered business and worked for one firm until he was twenty-three years old.

This was the most interesting period of his life. It was the time when his mind was active in every direction—as every boy's mind is active all the time if he is a healthy boy. It was a period during which great things were happening in the world of invention—things which influenced Frank's mind and unconsciously shaped his future life.

14

It is hard to believe, as you sit and talk with this successful business man with branches in New York, Berlin and Paris and his enormous business in all parts of the world, that he was the boy who made so much trouble for his teachers when he was in public school. Truant boys are not always bad boys. So it was with Frank Hornby. Sometimes boys are truants because their minds are so actively interested in something which they have no opportunity of getting. Sometimes they are truants because the teacher does not know how to talk to them or treat them. Sometimes they are truants because their school work is so distasteful. Sometimes they are truants because they have not been taught the fundamental principles which make all future study easier, whether it is in graded school, high school, college or university.

There are fundamentally correct ways of doing most things. If they are not done correctly, then everything that

15

grows out of them is wrong and difficult. That is one reason why Meccano, which Frank Hornby invented, has made such a marvelous success in all parts of the world, and why it has been so widely imitated. It is fundamentally correct in its mechanical principles. Any other constructional toy has to be an imitation if it is correct mechanically. If it is not correct mechanically, then it will not build correctly.

Frank Hornby; not a boy now but with two boys serving their country, one at the front in a regiment from which only three hundred returned out of eleven hundred at the end of the first six months of fighting; does not like to talk much about his school days. He says that most of the time he was either a truant or wanting to be a truant. But

16

that does not do him justice as his later life demonstrates.

Some boys are "bullies." Some boys are "sissies"; some boys are stingy; others are liberal; some are tricky and others are straightforward, honest, fair in all their dealings and in all their actions.

Frank was never inclined to athletics. Strange to say, though not liking school, he was a student and a great reader. Furthermore, he had a tender heart. He liked to read good books. He was greatly impressed by any book that told of the great achievements of the heroes and inventors of the world.

Thousands and thousands of American boys as well as English boys, and indeed boys of all countries, have been inspired by the books of that famous English writer, Samuel Smiles. He it was who wrote the book called *"Self Help."* He also wrote the book called *"Thrift."* Queen Victoria knighted him because of the wonderful influence he

17

had upon boys and men in all parts of the world through these inspiring books.

It must have been Frank's mother who gave him a copy of the book *"Self Help,"* because mothers have a way of putting good books in front of their boys and thereby influencing the boy's life for good, and honor, and ambition. At any rate, Frank read this marvelous book; that is, he read at it. It made such an impression on him that it was hard to read it right through as you would a regular story, because it so filled his imagination with the pictures of the great men of the world and of how they had struggled to achieve success that his eyes were filled with tears and his throat choked with the feelings that were trying to get out.

He was so moved that he read it over and over again. It set his ambition on fire. He, too, wanted to become a great inventor, a great manufacturer, a great leader—he wanted to succeed.

Possibly, too, the fact that during

Frank's school and early working days many of the world's most famous inventions were perfected, had an influence on his young mind and helped to shape the course which he was later to follow.

One of the greatest events in the history of human achievement was the invention of the steam engine. It has been said that the history of mechanical development counts forward or backward from the time of this invention.

With the building of the first steam engine a new era of invention began. This era of mechanical progress stretched over a number of years, and many marvelous inventions which followed reached the height of their development just at the time when Frank Hornby was most interested in reading about such things and most able to understand what a wonderful influence they would have on the world.

Undoubtedly, one of the most wonderful of all these inventions which were then coming to light was the electric incandescent lamp perfected by Thomas Edison, the great American Electrical Wizard. His installation of one hundred and fifty electric incandescent lamps on the steamship "Columbia" is regarded as the first practical electric illuminating plant in history.

Other famous inventors were doing great things at this time. Among them was Edward Weston, a pioneer who did much to lay the foundation of the present electrical industry; Alexander Graham Bell, who invented the telephone; J. P. Holland, whose early experiments with submarine boats gave the world many of the ideas which have so changed maritime warfare; Sir Hiram Maxim, who later invented the silencer for guns, at that time was just coming into prominence with his automatic, self-loading machine gun. These, and many more, famous geniuses who have given to the world inventions which have since become known to every boy in the land, were all working, and thinking, and planning, and studying, day and night, to realize their dreams.

Very true, in later years, other men —and a very great many of them were Americans—produced new inventions that have become just as well known as those which were brought out in Frank Hornby's early days. Among these more recent inventors are the Wright brothers, who made such remarkable progress in the development of the flying machine; Marconi—a young Italian— who invented the first practical wireless apparatus, the further development of which has made possible the sending of messages through the air clear across the Atlantic Ocean; George B. Selden, to whom has been credited the first experiment in this country with the gas vehicle —now the automobile. His first experiments are interesting. Almost every boy knows how an automobile is run. He knows that the power is secured by gas formed by mixing gasolene and air to-

21

gether and compressed inside of the cylinder and then exploded with an electric spark. But Selden was the first man in America who really worked out this principle successfully. He realized that the steam engine—before then other men had tried to run automobiles by steam—was entirely too heavy for the purpose and so he endeavored to produce a gas engine. At first he generated gas by burning the liquid fuel and tried to use the gas in the cylinder of his engine just as steam is used to-day. But he soon found that this was not practical, and finally decided that the power must come from the explosion of the gas in the cylinder itself.

But nothwithstanding these early experiments and inventions of Selden's, we should point to Chas. E. Duryea as the father of the American automobile. Strange to say, he started out at first with the idea of building a flying machine. Then he came across a gas engine; a crude one, but still a gas engine. It used gasolene for fuel and had **electric** ignition. He says that "It weighed a ton, at least, and was as big as a dinner table, while the gas tank"— which was the same as the carburetor on the automobile to-day—"was as big as a wash tub." It certainly must have been a funny looking gas engine.

Some time later he began the construction of his first motor carriage; it was completed and actually ran, and so to-day it is said that the first successful American gasolene automobile was built and run by Chas. E. Duryea.

Every boy to-day likes to read about inventions; the great struggles of famous inventors, and how they worked, suffered and persevered until they at last succeeded. Every boy is fascinated in reading about the development of the locomotive, and in seeing pictures of all the different locomotives that have been used.

So it was with Frank Hornby. All these wonderful inventions were written about in the newspapers, the magazines and the books during Frank Hornby's early business days. Is it any wonder that Frank, as he read about these men and their inventions, should dream of the time when he too would be a great inventor?

Every boy, whether he is American, English, German, French, Italian or whatever nationality he may be, is a born inventor. He instinctively wants to make something. He wants to use his hands. He wants to build, and to create things which are his very own. Many boys lose their interest in building and in creating and in constructing because they do not have the right material to work with. You never saw a healthy boy who didn't like to hammer and saw and build, but how often when he tries to hammer, he destroys or injures property and is scolded or punished for it, so he loses interest and all because he hasn't the right things to work with.

Frank Hornby had deep down in his

24

heart the desire to invent something which would be useful to boys in all countries; something with which they could build the things that they dreamed of building. He wanted to invent something which would be useful to boys in making their minds grow. Then when they became men, they could make use of the knowledge they had gained by using his invention when they were boys.

How well Frank succeeded, we shall learn from the succeeding chapters.

CHAPTER II.

FRANK HORNBY'S STRUGGLES AS AN INVENTOR.

Isn't it strange that almost every boy thinks of the hardest thing in the world when he wants to become an inventor? Frank Hornby's first attempt at invention was a machine that would give perpetual motion.

For a hundred years in every land and among every people, boys and men have been thinking about perpetual motion and what a marvelous thing it would be if they could create something that would give perpetual motion.

Reverently, boys, just stop to think that there is only one being who has ever created perpetual motion—He is God. The world keeps on turning on its own axis and also keeps moving perpetually around the sun.

What makes it go forward? What makes it whirl on its own axis?

We think of the world as a great place, a wonderful place. We talk about traveling around the world as if that were the most marvelous thing that could ever happen to anybody.

Yet scientists tell us that this world, the earth, is only one of hundreds and thousands, yes, millions of other planets, or "earths," which keep revolving around the sun, just as our earth does. We do not know whether there are boys on the other planets. We do not know whether they have inventors there, but we do know that they all move in their own circles around the sun and that the whole universe is governed by some divine force or natural law which seems to us mortals to be perpetual motion.

Every boy, every man, every human being has a spark of the Divine in him.

27

God is in each one of us; that is, each one has a soul, which is capable of desiring to be like God.

Possibly, that is why so many boys think of perpetual motion. They see the water running down the brook into the river and then into the ocean, drawn up out of the ocean by the sun's rays, blown back over the land in clouds driven by the wind, and rained down again upon the land to make the crops grow, and coming out of the land into the brook and down the brook into the river, down the river into the ocean again, continually from year to year, from age to age, running down, being drawn up and carried back, and running down again, forever and ever—a perpetual going and coming.

We see the Summer come and then the Autumn, and the leaves turn a beautiful golden red, and then Winter with snow and ice and Spring with the birds singing and the flowers breaking open and the planting being done. Then

Summer comes again. The older we grow, the faster the seasons seem to go by, but they always come back. Here also there seems to be a perpetual motion in the coming and going of the seasons.

If God created the clouds, the mountains, the land, the brooks and rivers and seas and if He created the Summer, the Autumn, the Winter and the Spring, and if He created the birds, the flowers, the fields and the grain and the cattle and man, then we, His children, with God in us, naturally think the same thoughts that He has thought and we naturally try to do the same things that He has done.

So that when Frank Hornby wanted to create perpetual motion, he was merely following his natural inclination to be a healthy boy and respond to the spirit of God that was working in him.

But, then he became a very practical boy immediately afterward. He next tried to invent something that would save him working so hard.

If you work on a farm, haven't you often wished that somebody would invent something that would milk the cows, so that you would not have to get up at four o'clock in the morning and have the old cow hit you in the head with her stub tail and kick you over and spill the milk on you and make you get whipped for spilling the milk, when she was trying to kick the flies? Now, lo and behold! Some inventor has made a milking machine, so that the machine does the milking while you can do something else, or go and play.

Haven't you as a boy wished that somebody would invent a machine that would chop the wood and bring it in, build the fire and carry out the ashes? Somebody has invented such a machine, for now we merely turn the button and we have electric fires, electric stoves, electric heaters, electric irons, electric coffee-pots.

Haven't you as a boy wished that somebody would invent some machine so that you would not have to hoe corn and potatoes and cabbages and get all hot, sweaty and tired out in the field, while other boys were playing baseball or going to the circus? Somebody has invented a cultivator, a mowing machine, a plow, a harvester, a driller, and a tractor to pull farm machinery and do many of the things that boys in olden days had to do.

Frank Hornby worked for a meat importer. England is a damp, foggy country. When bacon was piled up in the warehouses in great piles waiting to be distributed throughout the country to the small stores, the brine would drip from the bacon and run down leads or troughs to a pit or well in the center. This well would fill with brine.

One day Frank was told what a syphon was. So he immediately got a little tube, put one end in a glass of water, sucked on the other end and then

31

quickly put the end that was in his mouth down below the top of the water outside of the glass. Of course, the water all ran out of the glass.

Wasn't that a strange thing to a boy who had never seen such a thing happen before? How he must have wondered what made that water run up hill over the top of the glass and down the outside! Do you know what makes it do that? It is because there is a little more water in the tube outside of the glass than there is inside. As the water that is outside of the glass begins to fall, it forms a vacuum in the tube. Now a vacuum is a space where there is no air and as there are fifteen pounds of air pressure on each square inch of space all around us, that fifteen pounds pressing on the water in the glass forces it up into the tube and makes it run right up and does not let that vacuum exist. Now, since the water on the outside is continually falling, the vacuum continues to exist, and the water con-

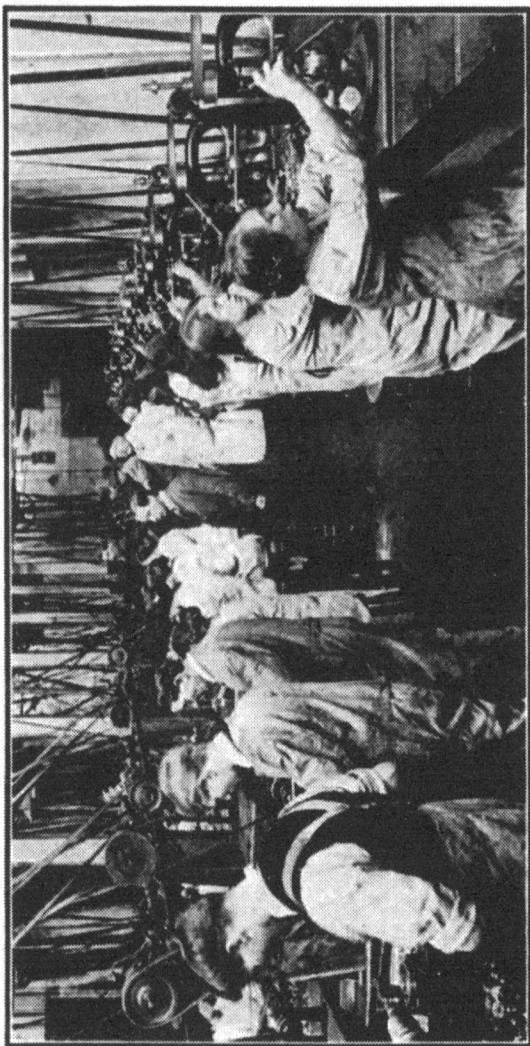

MACHINE SHOP IN PRESENT FACTORY.

tinues to run into the tube and up over the top and down, being forced by the fifteen pounds of atmospheric pressure after you have started the water running.

Imagine Frank's delight and enthusiasm and wild joy as he started to invent a syphon which would lift all of the brine out of the well automatically without his doing any work.

But that was a hard nut to crack!

New York City has spent almost two-hundred million dollars ($200,000,000) to build a new water System, bringing a vast river of pure water down from the Catskill Mountains. New York City is on the east side of the Hudson River. The Catskills are on the west side. The Hudson River itself is not pure drinking water. Therefore, this river of pure drinking water had to be brought either over or under the Hudson River. Furthermore, it was such a tremendous stream—it can supply New York with five hundred million (500,000,000) gallons of water a day—that it was almost impossible to think of pumping it over the river or under the river. Therefore, some system of syphoning had to be invented so that the water would automatically run under the Hudson River and up on the other side.

Before Frank could have syphoned the brine out of the pit in Liverpool, he would have had to get machinery for taking the air out of the tube that ran from the brine pit, and he would have had to dig a space outside of the brine pit and below the brine in the pit, so that it could fall and in that way suck up more brine over the top of the pit and out into a space lower on the outside.

Something like that is what the engineers did with the water for New York City. The great tube under the Hudson, just above West Point—where the United States Military Academy is located—goes 1,200 feet under the ground and then along through solid rock under

34

the Hudson River, then up on the other side. On the Catskill side of the river the Olive bridge dam was built. It is nearly a mile long; 220 feet high and 190 feet thick at the base. Behind this enormous dam is a lake, known as the Ashokan reservoir. This reservoir holds one hundred and thirty-two billion gallons of water (132,000,000,000). This great lake of pure water forms behind the enormous dam high up in the mountains. When it reaches the top, it falls by gravity out of this man-made lake into this great syphon under the river. It goes down to the bottom, across through the solid rocks and up the other side. But since the Catskill side is higher than the other side, the water is forced ever on and on until it reaches New York City. It is distributed through New York City in tubes which are 600 to 800 feet under the ground. It goes under the East River into Brooklyn and furnishes these great cities with an inexhaustible supply of pure water; a supply big enough for a city as big, or twice as big, as London.

Frank failed in his attempt to build an automatic syphon pumping device to empty the brine pit, but Samuel Smiles' books had taught him that failure was the most valuable thing in the world to teach a boy success.

Next, Frank got a workshop with the money that he had saved.

One of the first things for any boy to do who wants to succeed is to save some money so that he will have capital to work with. How marvelously has Samuel Smiles in his book *"Thrift"* described how the great successes in the world of business have come from thrift, from saving so that you will have capital to work with when you want to do your great work.

Frank Hornby bought tools for working with brass and other metals. He had to save a long time and he had to buy tools one at a time. All in all he spent a great deal of money in order to work with these tools. It took him years and years to save money enough to buy the tools to make the parts that have since become the Meccano System which any boy can buy for a very small price.

Every inventor is interested in making something which will be useful to the people among whom he lives. Eli Whitney made a cotton gin because he had traveled down South and knew that they needed a machine for taking the seeds out of cotton. In England the people ride to and fro in busses, just as in this country we do in street cars. So Frank spent weary weeks and months trying to invent a ticket box which would take the various shapes of metal checks which were required to record the various distances which passengers traveled. Such a box would save confusion and the extra labor of the conductor and be a convenience to the public.

But he was again doomed to disappointment.

As he failed, he went over his favorite book and read again of the great hero, the inventor of the process of glazing china, who, after almost everything else in the house had been broken up and used to build a fire to run the kiln, at last smashed his own bed-stead and afterwards slept on the floor. His determination to succeed was so strong that he used his bed-stead to increase the heat of his fire so he could melt the materials for glazing the chinaware. Think of the hardship, boys, of that man, Bernard Palissy, who suffered hunger and hardship and ridicule in order that we might enjoy the beautiful china of to-day.

So Frank Hornby knew that although he had failed two, or three, or four, or five times, yet there were the histories, the biographies of so many great men who had failed, and failed, and failed many more times than he had and yet who were the world's heroes to-day because they had kept on and on, until at last they achieved success.

How beautiful is that poem representing Columbus, telling his sailors day after day to

"Sail on and on and on."

When they muttered and objected, his command was to "Sail on and on and on."

When they threatened mutiny and were determined to kill him if he did not turn back, he finally had to trust in God and tell them to "Sail on" for one more day, anyway.

Think of the hero with the divine faith that he could discover a passage to the wealth and the glory of the East Indies by going westward, fighting, even almost deceiving his sailors, to make them go on and on westward just "one more day."

No wonder that when he came to the land which he thought was the wealthy East Indies, but which in reality held in the future, ten, yes hundreds of times the wealth of the East Indies—no wonder that he was looked upon as almost divine.

Any boy, any man, any human being who perseveres, who feels down deep in his heart that he is right, who is willing to sacrifice comfort, friendship, immediate success, ease, popularity, admiration, everything that we all like, in order that he can keep on and on and on until he accomplishes the thing that he sets out to do—that man is almost divine.

In 1861, only two years before Frank Hornby was born, Kansas was admitted as one of the States of our Union, and took as its motto "Ad Aspera Per Asperum," meaning "To the stars through difficulty." That in reality was Frank Hornby's motto. Indeed! That is the unconscious motto of every ambitious boy, be his skin white or black, brown or yellow, in this land or any other land.

CHAPTER III.

THE LONG YEARS.

Then came the years of trial. None but a strong, stout heart could have endured and come through successfully after such waiting.

Frank's father died. His business was closed out. Frank went to work for another provision house.

The new firm imported American beef and meat and other food products from Armour & Company, Swift & Company and Morris & Company, the great Chicago, Omaha and Kansas City packers. For twenty-one long years Frank Hornby worked for this firm. He went there to work when he was twenty-four.

Being a good singer, having a fine tenor voice, he was much sought after by church choirs. That brought him into contact with other musicians, and it was there that he met his wife-to-be.

Meanwhile, Frank had become very much interested in the "Band of Hope" movement.

In England, the "Band of Hope" is a temperance society, just as the White Ribbon is a temperance society in America.

At first, the other boys made fun of him, and told him that he was no "goody-goody," and why should he be prominent in the "Band of Hope"?

But as opposition always strengthens a strong boy, this ridicule of his pals merely made him more determined to make his work in the "Band of Hope" successful.

So he went to work. He provided entertainment for the boys until finally he had a "Band of Hope" society of over three hundred boys, although he was little more than a boy himself.

We think of the English as not having a sense of humor. Nevertheless, his great success in this "Band of Hope" work was due to his keen sense of humor, to his enjoyment of good fun. Hence he mixed in with his comrades and his organized pleas for temperance, and for clean living, and for right thinking, and for conscientious doing, combined with entertainment of a clean sort, kept the rooms of his "Band of Hope" society packed on every open night.

Sometimes the minister, being a little old and a little severe, would scowl at the entertainment that was given; sometimes he would object to the entertainers that were brought in from the outside, but nevertheless Frank Hornby was the ruling spirit and the real power in making this "Band of Hope" society in his church a great success which was long afterward spoken of.

In this way he developed his ability as an organizer and gained experience which was useful to him in later years. Every boy should strive to develop his

44

ability as an organizer, and should, by actual practice among his comrades, try to gain their confidence and induce them to make him their leader. By doing so he will acquire the power to lead men when he grows up.

As the years went on, he was married. A son was born, then another son.

Mr. Hornby, as he was then called, was looked upon as settled in his business. He had a trusted position with the firm of meat importers.

Yet he was a boy at heart. He had never lost his interest in inventors, and in the desire to invent something which would be useful, amusing, and at the same time teach boys things which would be valuable for them to know. Nights and holidays he kept busy in his little work shop.

How often do we look around us and see men thirty years old who seem to be tinkering away over some useless thing which we do not understand. We laugh at them. We poke fun at them to other people, yet so many times these same men are living through hardships which would call for our real sympathy and admiration if we knew how b r a v e l y they were sticking to their tasks to a c c o m p l i s h the things which they set out to a c c o m p l i s h when they were boys.

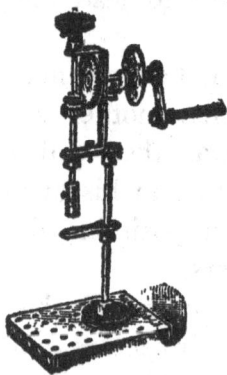

"Mike" Murphy— the greatest athletic trainer that America has ever produced— the man who trained the American teams that won the Olympic victories abroad, the man who became famous as the trainer of the great Yale football teams and later of the great Pennsylvania track teams —used to say "No matter how tired you are, remember that the other fellow is just as tired. If you think that you are 'all in,' remember that the other fellow is also just ready

46

to drop. If you think that you cannot take another step, grit your teeth and keep going, make a sprint even though it kills you, because that will take the heart out of your competitors. Never say die, never quit even though you are beaten. You can't tell what may happen. Even though you believe that you are beaten, you may not be; something may turn up, which will affect your competitor and let you come in ahead after all. Keep fighting every inch of the way clear to the tape."

Frank Hornby kept fighting every inch of the way clear to the tape. He thought before he reached the goal that he was beaten, but trying to think of something that would please his own little boys at last showed him the way to realize his ambitions.

He was on a train going quite a long journey to visit his relatives. His wife and his two boys had gone on ahead. He was wondering what he could give them for Christmas. They too had been interested in working in his little shop and in seeing him work.

As he sped along on the journey, he did what all boys and most men do. He gazed out of the window, watching the scenery, and the various buildings and everything else of interest, as the train flew past.

As he rumbled over the bridges, and saw the great derricks and cranes at work in building operations and saw the wagons and the various machines, and the factories along the way, he began to dream how as a boy he had so wanted to build a bridge, how he had wanted to build a crane which could lift

ELECTRO-PLATING SHOP IN PRESENT FACTORY.

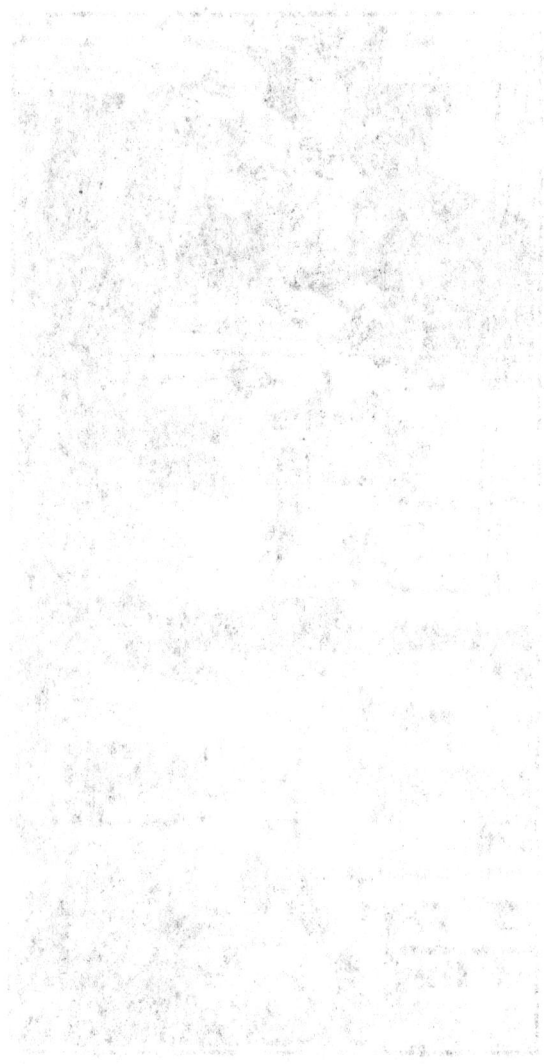

things and swing them around and put them down somewhere else. How he had wanted to build an engine that would move, and that would pull a train of cars. How he had wanted to build a bridge that he could run his cars over, and O Joy! a bridge that the steamboats would come up to and whistle and the man in the tower of the bridge would toot, toot his O. K. closing the bridge to railroad traffic, and then the bridge would slowly turn around and let the steamboats go through and then would toot, toot again and swing back into place and let the patient engineer of the freight train go on across with his loaded cars. Frank Hornby was once a boy and knew what boys like.

As he journeyed on, he began to wonder how he could make a toy that would amuse his boys and at the same time give them useful instruction that would be valuable to them when they grew up. He knew the fascination that boys have for machinery, for inventing, and for anything of a mechanical nature, and he also knew the pleasure all boys get out of taking something to pieces and building it up again. But to his practical mind, this seemed to be a negative or backwards training. So he thought how much better it would be if he could invent something that would make the boys think how to construct it, instead of how to tear it apart. He thought what a wonderful thing it would be if he could invent something with which a boy could build a train, or an engine, or a steamboat, or a bridge, or a windmill, or a railroad crane, or a locomotive, or any of the other fascinating mechanical things at which a boy stands in awe.

But what do you suppose was the first thing he thought of building? He says it is the thing which almost every

50

boy wants to build first. It was a crane, or derrick. Why do you suppose it is that a boy is so interested in a crane? Why is it that a boy will never get tired of watching a crane?

Don't you suppose it is because every boy wants to be strong? Has he not read and been told about Samson and about all of the other great heroes who were mighty warriors and great, strong men; and as a little boy is he not always trying to lift things which nearly break his back, but which he is not able to budge?

But how was he going to do it? After once getting the idea, he took out a pencil and paper and began to figure what could be done. He made little sketches of cranes. He thought, and thought, and thought, and at last an inspiration came to him. It flashed into his mind that if he could make metal strips of varying lengths and with some kind of a fastening to hold them together, these strips could be held

51

in position to form the crane he was trying to build.

Strange as it may seem, Frank Hornby, although a poor student
in mathematics, had always
been mechanical and mathe-
matical in his calculations.
Possibly if he had had the
right incentive and proper
training as a boy, he would
have been a great mathema-
tician.

At least, his mind worked
logically. He began to figure
that if these strips were one-
half inch wide and of three
different lengths—2½ inches
long, 5½ inches long and
12½ inches long—and if
each strip had holes punched
down the center, also one-half inch
apart, and arranged so that one hole
came right in the center and there were
an equal number each side of it so that
when two strips were overlapped, they

could be fitted together so as to form a longer strip, a boy could use these strips to build a crane in a way that would interest and instruct him.

All the old inventive genius in him awoke. He kept puzzling and figuring and working enthusiastically over this problem, until he was almost carried past the station where he was going to visit his family and relatives.

Gathering up his things, he hurriedly tumbled out of his compartment—for in England they have compartments in the trains, and not a long row of seats as in our American passenger cars—just in time to save himself from a bad fall as the train was gaining headway.

Frank could hardly wait to get back home and into his little work shop. He obtained plain strips of copper, since copper is a soft metal and easy to work with, and set to work to build the strips in accordance with the little sketches he had made on the train.

After he got them made, then came

the question of how he could fasten them together. This was easily solved where he wanted to join one strip to another in order to make a longer strip. But when he wanted to fasten two strips together et right angles, he had to do still more planning. He accomplished this by making an angle bracket with a hole in each side, so that the strips could be fastened together with it.

He knew that to interest boys his new invention should be fastened together as nearly like a real crane as he could make it, so he decided to use real little nuts and bolts for this purpose.

But where would he get at a small cost the little nuts and bolts for fastening these strips together? That also was a problem—to get the right kind of nuts and bolts. Finally in desperation he had to make them himself. Then he was able to take the strips which he himself had cut out and made, with his two little boys enthusiastically helping him, and

54

commence to actually put together the crane he had planned.

After Frank had put together the framework for his new crane, he found that he needed a pulley wheel for the jib and also some wheels for the crane itself, so that he could move it backwards and forwards and around when it was carrying a load. He also found that he needed some spindles, or rods, which would fit into the holes in the strips and on which he could place the wheels. So he went to a brass foundry with a pattern which he had carefully worked out and had the pulleys, flanges and bush wheels made as he wanted them. Then he got a clock maker to make him some cog wheels so that one would fit into the other. A little wheel into a big one, and the big one into a little one again, so that by turning a handle and applying

55

a little power to the smallest wheel, he could raise ten or twenty times the weight which was represented by the power exerted on the handle.

You have often seen two men turning the crank at a big crane or derrick. They turn the handle around and around and wind a rope or chain over a spindle, lifting a big rock, or a timber or a steel girder or even a big safe that weighs many times what the men do; lifting it slowly but surely until it gets where they want it.

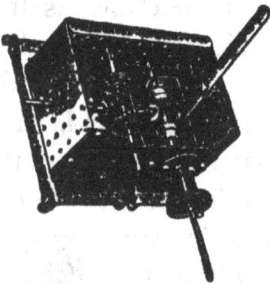

Frank wanted a crank handle—so he bent one of the rods to form such a handle—and you will find in every Meccano outfit to-day one of these bent rods which is used as a crank handle.

When the first model of this first crane was completed, with its solid base and

56

its long jib running up in the air, with the long cord running up to the pulley at the top of the jib and through the pulley down to the gear wheels; with the weights fastened to the hook attached to the other end of the cord, and the little crank in the base that could be turned and the weight lifted and the jib of the crane turned around and lowered so as to deposit the weight in any other place— when this first model was finally finished, just think what joy came into that household.

Frank Hornby was at last an inventor—he had invented something amusing, instructive, and educational. He had made something that his boys never wanted to stop play-

57

ing with; something which boys all over the world would be just as crazy to play with.

But little did Frank Hornby think, as he admired his new invention, that a feature of far greater importance than anything he had yet discovered, was just ahead of him waiting for his alert mind to grasp it. His crane to him was wonderful—but it was nothing as compared to the greater discovery he was on the threshold of making.

He admired his crane, his boys played with it, and after a time Frank decided that he would take it apart. So he removed the jib and the upper parts, leaving only the base with its four wheels. Then the wonderful feature that has made Meccano far more amusing, useful and instructive than any other constructional toy occurred to him. When he had removed the jib and the other upper parts of his crane, he discovered

that he had left a small, four wheeled truck, and that by taking the strips of metal that had formed the jib, and fastening them together in another way, he could make a railroad track on which his four-wheel truck could run. He got to thinking still further, to figuring and experimenting, and before very long he had used those same strips to make a small wheelbarrow, a little wagon, a

chair and a table and many other simple little things of that kind.

It was wonderful how all these years of working and thinking and dreaming seemed to gather together and pour all of their experience into this new toy.

His active mind commenced to work

all over again. He saw visions of great immense bridges, steam and electric loco-motives, railroad trains, automobiles, windmills, saw mills, derricks, pile driv-ers and hundreds—yes thousands—of different great machines and structures that boys were always marveling at, all of which could be reproduced in a small size with the various length strips, angle brackets, nuts and bolts, rods, wheels, gears and pulleys that he had first used in the construction of that simple little crane.

This inter-change-ability feature of Frank Hornby's new invention required further thought, and more planning, but Frank quickly saw its immense possibili-ties, and also saw that in order to have all his parts interchangeable, the holes would have to be all the same size, all the same distance apart, all placed in the same position on every part that he was to use. To say it in just a little differ-ent way, all the parts should be inter-changeable—they should be constructed so they could be changed around and used in more different ways. That is what makes Meccano such an amusing, interesting and instructive toy. It is because all the parts are interchangeable so that you can use the same parts in many different ways and build so many more different things. Of course, this was only the beginning of the idea, but it has developed to such a great extent that to-day the boy who owns a Meccano

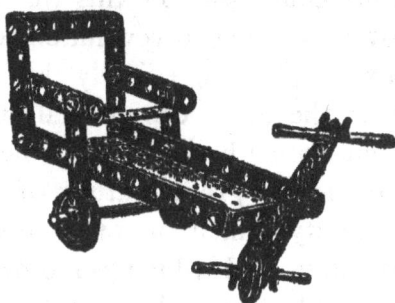

outfit can build a working model of any mechanical, electrical or structural machine or structure he has ever seen. And furthermore, the models he can build closely resemble the actual machines or

61

structures, because soon after Frank's first experiments with copper strips, he discovered that if he used strips of shining steel instead, they would be stronger, and would build bigger and stronger things, and would more closely resemble the big steel girders and beams that real engineers and contractors use. And so strips of shining steel are furnished to-day in every Meccano outfit.

Of course, at the beginning, nobody but Frank could see how this wonderful new toy was going to revolutionize toys for boys. He immediately began to dream of the great commercial success that would come because of his new invention and its great feature of interchange-ability which no other toy had at that time, and which no other toy has been able to match since then.

There it was, the dream of all his years—but how his dream had grown, how by starting out to make a simple little toy, he had by being determined and sticking to it, invented a toy, or a

62

machine, or a plaything, or a useful article—whatever you want to call it—which his own boys were absolutely crazy to play with and which all boys all over the world would in time learn to play with and save their pennies to buy. But at that time, he just had his model. The real problem was how to make more models and more parts and in such a way that he could sell them and make money from them and make a success of his invention.

CHAPTER IV.

HOW FRANK HORNBY PATENTED AND PROTECTED HIS INVENTION.

Although his close friends who saw this little model were dubious as to its success, nevertheless Frank Hornby consulted a patent attorney, or "agent" as they are called in England, and got him to make a very diligent search to ascertain if any patent for anything of a similar kind had ever been granted before.

In Great Britain, at the present time the application for a patent is made, and then the government posts a bulletin of the application for four months. This is in reality a notice to all contenders to file their prior claim to the right to such a patent if they have such claims, otherwise the patent will be granted at the end of the probation period.

As the probation time for Frank Hornby's patent drew to a close it was evident that nobody else had ever applied for or been granted a patent similar to this one for Meccano. The British Government granted Frank his patent in January of 1901.

In the United States also, the government patent office makes a very thorough and diligent search to see whether other inventors have been granted a patent or filed an application for a patent before they grant any patent to an inventor.

At the present time Frank Hornby has patents on Meccano—which is no longer looked on merely as a toy—in Great Britain and its Colonies, the United States, Germany, Italy and many other countries.

All bright boys know that a patent is a very valuable thing for an inventor to acquire if after he has gotten it he knows

65

how to get some manufacturing concern to manufacture this article, or is able to organize a company to do his own manufacturing.

The civilized countries of the world say that an inventor is entitled to protection for a term of years for any valuable invention, particularly if it is useful to m a n k i n d, and grant him a patent p r o t e c t i n g him against infringement. This is because all governments recognize that an inventor may spend years and years of his life, working for the good of humanity, without getting very much pay unless his invention is protected for a number of years while he is getting it started.

If the governments of the world are so fair to inventors, then every boy who believes in fair play, and believes that a boy or man who has worked for years to invent something should enjoy the right to that invention and the profits which it might bring to him, should ask for Frank Hornby's Meccano, whenever he wants to buy a Meccano outfit.

He should not merely ask for a constructional toy or a builder, or an erecting toy, but should ask for Meccano. There is only one Meccano, although there are some careless and unscrupulous people who call any constructional toy a Meccano toy, just as there are some people who will call any camera a "Kodak" or any flashlight an "Eveready" or any dollar watch an "Ingersoll." However, if you look for the word "Meccano" and be sure that it is made by the company of which Frank Hornby is now President, then there will be no way of fooling you, no infringers can get your money for an imitation of Meccano. You can get what you want—one orig-

inal, constructional toy which is founded
on absolutely correct mechanical principles, and which has greater inter-change-
ability of parts, and which, therefore, requires far fewer parts to build the
greatest number of different things, and
which will make an unlimited variety
of models.

CHAPTER V.

ORGANIZING THE COMPANY TO MAKE THE TOY.

You can cut out enough strips yourself to make a small model. You can keep pegging away until you have made quite a supply of strips, and you might even make screws, and nuts, and rods, and wheels, and pulleys, and other things for building such an outfit; but it takes money to rent a factory building, no matter how small, and get the tools to make goods on a large enough scale so that they can be sold and earn a profit.

Frank Hornby soon found out that after he had invented his toy the hardest problem of his life confronted him.

Thousands and thousands of good inventions have been made which are never heard of because the inventor was not a good enough business man, and did not have a character which made people have confidence enough in him, to invest money in his invention or loan him, personally, money for carrying on his work of manufacturing and selling.

Thanks to early Christian training, clean living, right thinking, thrift, and a conscience that kept him true and strong under all temptations and hardships, Frank Hornby had developed a character which to-day the American bankers call "the finest kind of a financial risk."

In order that he should not be compelled to ask men to invest or loan money wholly on his own judgment, Frank Hornby submitted photographs and drawings of his model to the distinguished scientist, Dr. Hele-Shaw, Professor of Engineering at the Walker Engineering Laboratories, University College, Liverpool. Professor Hele-Shaw was not only a kindly man, but he was also a very wise man, and a great scientist. As soon as he studied these photographs and drawings he saw that here was a toy which was not only very interesting, but extremely educational. He saw that no boy could play with Frank Hornby's Meccano without being trained in the principles of engineering. He saw that a boy could learn unconsciously the great principles of me-chanics from this little toy. The boy could learn the principles of an arch, just such an arch as is used in all bridge w o r k, and in the gables of the roofs of houses and buildings, and in other forms of building construction. By putting these little Meccano parts together he quickly saw that this Meccano toy could teach boys the principle of the inclined plane, the principle of the pulley, where

71

a man can pull up several times his own weight by the use of pulleys.

He grew enthusiastic because his life had been spent in educating engineers, and he saw that boys could, while playing, now learn the principles which he worked so hard to teach grown men.

It is so hard to understand what people mean when they go into a long explanation. You do not follow them through, and after a while do not really know what they are talking about.

How often the teacher in school will try to explain an example, and you will sit and look at her and try to listen, but after a while will not know what she means, or what she wants you to understand.

Many grown people are like boys in this respect. That is why all systems of education have changed in recent years.

Froebel has become a name honored all over the world because he discovered the kindergarten method of letting little folks play at games which make the kindergarten interesting; in that way making children want to go to school, instead of wanting to play truant.

Froebel's work has changed a great deal of the educational system of the public schools. In the book called *"Froebel's Occupations,"* Herbert Spencer, the great English educator, is quoted as saying, "Almost invariably children show a strong tendency * * * to make, to build; a propensity which, if duly encouraged and directed, will not only prepare the way for scientific conceptions, but will develop those powers of manipulation in which most people are so deficient."

Horace Mann has become an honored name all over the world because he went a step further than Froebel and taught boys and girls too big for kindergarten, too big even sometimes for graded schools, how to do things with their hands, how to work in carpenter shops, and art studios, and mills and printing offices, and all kinds of places where

73

they will have to work when they get
out of school and start to earning their
own living. His system of teaching has
developed into our present Manual
Training Schools. He was such a great
educator that he has influenced many of
the public schools.

Only recently a professor at Yale University, in an article published in the
Century Magazine, was bewailing the
fact that the whole tendency in American education was to study and do practical things rather than classical things.
The scientific schools are growing in enrollment everywhere, while the classical
schools are falling off in enrollment or
are just able to hold their own. That
shows that the kindergarten idea of
Froebel, and the manual training idea
of Horace Mann, and the technical work
of Stevens, and the founders of such
great schools as the Massachusetts Institute of Technology, Pratt Institute in
Brooklyn, the Carnegie Institute of Pitts-
burg, and other great schools of that

kind, are getting a stronger and stronger hold on the young men and women of America.

Professor Hele-Shaw was himself a famous inventor, a dreamer in educational matters; he wrote back to Frank Hornby a very interesting letter telling him how pleased he was with his Meccano photographs and models, and saying that they were as good as a fairy story, and that as soon as Frank had them for sale, be sure to let him buy a set for his little boy.

What a fine thing it was to write a letter of that kind to this struggling inventor!

With that letter Frank Hornby was able to interest some men in putting money into a small manufacturing business for the purpose of manufacturing Meccano and putting it on the market so that every boy could have an outfit to play with.

CHAPTER VI.

FRANK HORNBY'S FIRST FACTORY.

Could it be called a "factory"? A picture of this one room with Frank Hornby's one assistant, a girl, is shown opposite this page. The picture shows this one assistant packing the new toys in boxes. Compare it with the picture of the present packing room, with its hundreds of girls, following page 107.

Frank Hornby with the little money that he had gathered together, rented a small room in Liverpool, and hired one girl to help him. He had made all of his patterns and went to different factories and had the various parts for his Meccano made. He had so little capital that practically none of the factories wanted to bother with such small

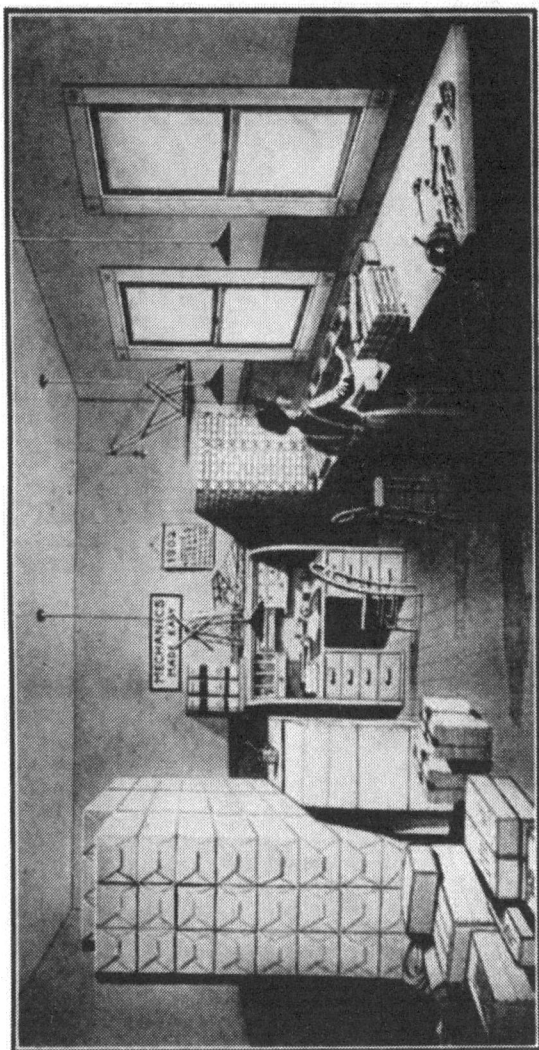

FRANK HORNBY'S FIRST FACTORY.

orders as he could give. It was only because of his earnestness and sincerity, and faith in the future of his invention, that the factories, out of sympathy and consideration for him, would bother to make the parts which were ordered in such small quantities that they would not be profitable for them to manufacture.

A great many business men will help a boy or young man who shows the spirit of Frank Hornby, even though they lose money in trying to help him. They think back over the days when they were struggling and trying to get ahead, and think of some kind man who gave them a helping hand, and their hearts are softened, and their sympathies awakened, and so they want to lend a helping hand to the deserving, struggling young beginners.

Frank Hornby saw that the parts were manufactured properly, and had them all sent to his little one room factory, where he and the girl who assisted him,

77

put them into boxes, and then took those boxes around from one store to another to sell them in order to get the money to manufacture more.

At first only one store in all of Liverpool would handle this new constructional toy. They handled it because they were an educational house. Their name was P h i l i p, Son & Nephew. The leading member of this firm was Mr. Tom Philip, a man of sound business judgment. He appreciated the merit of Meccano even in its first crude form and gladly lent his great influence to help make Meccano a success. They took up the sale of Meccano because of the letter which Professor Hele-Shaw wrote to Frank Hornby.

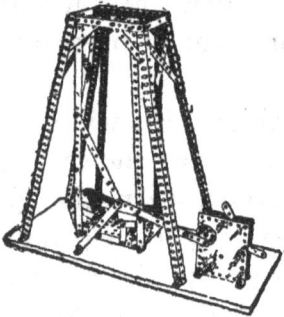

This firm sold, the first year, a few

78

outfits only, and in fact some of those were purchased by friends who knew how hard Hornby had worked to get his little enterprise started.

But the one big thing which was learned was, that those who bought Meccano and let their boys play with it, came back for more parts because the boys wanted to build bigger and always bigger things, and needed more parts to work with.

That was the one thing that Frank Hornby was sure of from the very beginning, although other people doubted his wisdom. He felt sure that any boy, anywhere, had in his own heart enough inventive, creative natural inclination, so that, if he were put down in a desert, or a forest, or locked up in a dungeon, with these little strips, and wheels and rods, and screws, and pulleys, he could be happy because he could satisfy his own desires to build something interesting and difficult and in that way to grow in skill as a real engineer.

His judgment was proved to be sound.

In the first Meccano outfits that were sold, the book of instructions showed only a few models. As you pick up the big, thick book of instructions which now goes with every original Meccano outfit, you cannot help but smile as you think of the little, thin, first Meccano book.

This big book of instructions which the boy gets to-day is filled from cover to cover with all kinds of interesting models which boys have built. But the models shown in this book are not a hundredth part of the models that have been built and submitted by boys in America, Great Britain, France and Germany, Australia, Italy, Russia, Turkey and every part of the world. In fact, the number of models that can be built from Meccano is unlimited.

THE FIRST FACTORY

Architects are now learning this fact, and are using Meccano for building models to submit when they are trying to get a contract for buildings or bridges, or other constructional work for which they are submitting drawings and plans.

So great has been the demand for Meccano amongst other inventors, that Frank Hornby's company now manufactures an Inventor's Accessory Outfit, so that an inventor can put together

these various parts of Meccano and build a model of the piece of machinery or the article that he is working on, and in that way experiment with a practical, working design before he goes to the great expense of building a real model of his invention. In taking this action, Frank Hornby shows his big heart, in going out to help other inventors who, like himself, are struggling to get ahead, just as he did through all the years when he was trying to make Meccano a success.

After the new outfits for Christmas, 1902, had been sold, it was learned that a great many more sets would be required for the next Christmas. Consequently a much larger number of Meccano outfits were prepared for Christmas, 1903. Messrs. Philip, Son & Nephew quickly sold out their 1903 supply.

The other toy dealers woke up to the fact that this new constructional toy was going to be a great success. They had so many boys and parents asking for it, that they commenced to buy it. In a short time, Frank Hornby could not supply the demand for his new constructional toy.

The business grew so rapidly in the next four or five years that it was almost as much of a hardship to supply the demand as it formerly had been to invent Meccano.

82

Because there were so many things to do, so many things to pay out money for, so many new ideas to incorporate, in order to make the outfit better each year, and there were so many salaries to pay to do the work over the whole twelve months when the business was all done, in those days, in the months of November and December.

Sometimes it seemed as if the strain was too great, that the business would never get up to that point where Frank could make enough in November and December to pay all the manufacturing, and selling, and living expenses for the other ten months, and still show a profit. It was not long before Frank Hornby was paying people who worked for him higher salaries than he himself drew.

But that is the way with the man who has invented something, and whose heart is in his work. His whole heart was in Meccano. He would have kept on with that manufacturing even though

83

he had to go outside and work to get money enough to carry it on.

It was his "pet," his "hobby."

It was like a child to him, which he could not and would not desert.

But his friends stood by him until the tide was turned and the business began to show constantly increasing profits.

Nor did those friends lose, because they shared in the profits when the business became a great success. Nobody can be around Frank Hornby today without realizing the bigness of his heart. His Berlin, Germany, branch had developed so rapidly that it was doing business not only throughout Germany, but in Austria, Italy, Russia, Turkey, and all through that part of Europe. It was a great business. The literature for the Berlin office had to be printed in twelve different languages. The salesmen who went out to call on the dealers and sell them Meccano had to be able to speak five or six different languages.

When the war broke out, all of this

business was confiscated, that is, taken right over by the German Government.

Yet, in telling about it, Frank Hornby did not express a single regret over his financial loss. He seemed to be very much distressed, however, because the English manager of his Berlin office had been interned—which is another way of

saying "locked up"—as an "enemy" of Germany. That was the thing about which Frank Hornby was worrying. His heart went out to the man who had been helping him build up the business in that part of Europe. He did not think so much about the lost business as he did about the hardship, humiliation, and suffering which the man—his employee, but in reality his friend—was undergoing in Berlin.

85

CHAPTER VII.

HOW FRANK HORNBY'S TOY GREW INTO A WORLD-WIDE INDUSTRY.

In 1903 the two rooms which had been required in place of the one little room in which the business had started, were not nearly big enough, so larger quarters were rented.

Then it was that Frank Hornby decided that he should make all of his parts himself, instead of having different manufacturers make the different parts.

This meant more trouble and more struggle to get the capital to buy the costly machinery for making the parts. Cutting out and stamping metal is a difficult work. It requires experience in manufacturing.

In the great metal manufacturing

plants in America, there are always a great many machines which are built to order to do the particular kind of work which is required in each factory. In a new industry like the manufacture of Meccano there were no machines ready for doing such work, so they had to be invented. Some of the machines used now are pictured in this book.

However, the problems of manufacturing were finally conquered, and in another short space of time still larger quarters were required.

At length Frank Hornby bought a piece of land containing two hundred and sixteen thousand square feet, that is, about five acres, and commenced the building of a big factory, so that the business could be arranged in departments and properly organized. You see in the front of this book, a picture of the great factory which now stands on this ground in Liverpool.

It is a wonderful tribute to the boy— grown now to be a man—who spent all his life in trying to invent something that would be useful to boys and men; a tribute to the boy who as a man did invent a toy, a useful, practical toy, that has endeared him to millions of boys all over the world.

What a satisfaction it must be to-day to Frank Hornby as he looks back over the years of his struggle and sees everywhere in the world men and boys playing with Meccano; building their trains, automobiles, locomotives, bridges, Ferris wheels, Eiffel towers, safes, weaving looms, sewing machines, clocks, derricks of all kinds, trolley cars, farming machines, wire making machines, dredges, printing presses, steam shovels, swinging boats, armored motor cars, drilling machines, elevators, sky scraper buildings, pile drivers, wind-mill pumps and thousands of other mechanical, electrical and constructional models that can be made with Meccano, and when made, can be operated just like the real ones

Even future Kings and Princes all

over the world play with Meccano. Scientific schools use Meccano for illustrating the principles of engineering and mechanics.

Of all the praise that has come to Frank Hornby because of his great invention, there is one letter out of many thousands which has deeply affected him. This is a letter from the parents of a poor, little bed-ridden boy who had an incurable disease and who all his life had to lie in bed. The father wrote something like this:

DEAR MECCANO:

I cannot tell you how grateful I am to you for the joy that you have given my poor little boy and that you have given to me, because of my boy's pleasure in Meccano.

He must lie in bed day after day. He has an active mind. He is thinking all the time about the great things that he will build when he gets well. He does not know —poor little fellow—that he will probably never be well. He does not know what the doctor does—that he is gradually failing and will not be with us very much longer.

But he works hour after hour over his Meccano, building his bridges, his trestles, his locomotives, his automobiles and his railroad tracks, his machines, and when night comes, he is tired out, but happy, and sleeps and rests so much better than he did before.

He thinks more of his Meccano than any little girl ever could think of her baby dolls; he can't bear to have it out of his sight, so we keep it on a chair right beside his bed all the time.

You have given my little boy so much happiness that I know you must have given a whole ocean of happiness to the other boys all over the world who play with Meccano. I think you have done a wonderful thing by inventing a toy which gives so much pleasure to those who play with it, and at the same time teaches the boy all about the principles of mechanics, which are so hard for him to learn when he tries to study the dry books.

My little boy can tell me about the principle of the lever, the principle of the bell crank, the principle of the pulley, the principle of gearing, what a suspension bridge is, how a dredge works, what a derrick does and lots of other things he has learned by playing with Meccano.

How wonderful it must be as a training for strong, healthy boys who some day will go out into the big world to be the engineers who will build the bridges, the buildings, the railroad stations, the tunnels, the subways, and the battleships.

I think that the man who invented a toy of this kind, which not only gives so much pleasure, but is so educational, should be honored by his own country in an unmistakable way.

Wouldn't you be proud of that kind of a letter?

Wouldn't you be proud if you had invented something which was so useful and so practical that a West African missionary should find a King of one of the savage tribes playing with it, and trying to learn these principles of modern building, of modern mechanics, in order that he could lead his ignorant people into the ways of civilization and teach them the things that even small boys in the great civilized world know?

CHAPTER VIII.

FRANK HORNBY'S
FURTHER INVENTIONS.

During all the years when Meccano was being built up as a business, Frank Hornby was not idle as an inventor. He was continually experimenting, continually working to invent other parts of Meccano, which would improve and enlarge the system. In that way, he adopted the worm wheel and the contrate wheel, which make it possible for boys to get so many more interesting arrangements of gears; the single bent strip; the crank, the coupling, the perforated rectangular plate, the sector plate, spring motor, and the wide girder strip.

The Meccano spring motor, shown below, is a wonderful little power plant that will run many of the mechanical things that boys build. It will run an automobile, a derrick, a swing, like the one on page 78, or most anything that does not require continuous power. It has a big, strong spring with a key that winds it easily; a starting and stopping brake, and a reversing lever. Very many different arrangements of gearing can be built on it, as it has the Meccano equidistant holes around the edge on each side.

Then the Meccano Girder Strip, on page 95, another of Frank Hornby's recent inventions, helps boys build large things. It is wider than any of the other strips and enables the boy to build big towers and bridges and sky-scraper buildings and other things quicker, easier, and more like the real ones.

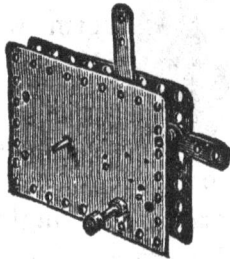

As these new inventions were added to the Meccano outfit, the adaptability of Meccano was of course enormously increased, yet there was one thing which was always kept in mind, and which to-day is strictly adhered to. That one thing is that every new part must maintain the principles of inter-change-ability. Furthermore, this meant at the beginning, and means to-day, that Meccano is in reality mechanical, electrical and structural engineering in miniature. A boy could never learn incorrect mechanical principles from playing with Meccano.

Everything that he learns from playing with Meccano will some day be useful to him in understanding engineering, and constructional mechanics, no matter whether he ever becomes an engineer or not. Everything that he learned by playing with Meccano will help him about his home or in his business. It will give him the knowledge that will be a power to him and will help in his future success.

As a result of the strict adherence to these mechanical principles—and there can never be more than one set of correct mechanical principles—the boys who play with Meccano have their ingenuity, their power of initiative and their imagination developed so that they do not need to always follow the models in the book of instruction, but can start out boldly after a little experience and draw their plans and invent and build newer and bigger models.

Ingenious boys can build all kinds of things with Meccano. Not long ago, a boy submitted the model of a weaving machine on this page and sent a necktie which he had woven with it. Any boy who has ever seen a weaving loom, of which there are a vast number in America, will immediately see how practical

PRESS DEPARTMENT PRESENT FACTORY.

this little Meccano model weaving machine really is.

Surely this boy must have seen an actual weaving machine. Perhaps he saw pictures of them in books or some one told him about them; or perhaps he went on a trip through the great weaving centers of this country and learned all about these wonderful looms.

Who knows how he got the idea of making a loom? But he has made it, and a wonderful little machine it is. He displayed such ingenuity and inventive genius that he won a part of the first cash prize offered by Meccano for the best models. Don't you think that this boy feels very proud of his weaving machine and of his winning that prize in a competition with other boys all over the world? And don't you see how, by the work he has done in building this machine, he has learned not only the ways of constructing a loom, but also the principles of loom weaving? Who can tell but what he will be at the head of a million dollar weaving mill some day? And just think of the fun he had building his loom!

A little French boy who lives in Nancy, France, made a wonderful clock which will run just like a big clock— and keep good time too. For centuries back the Swiss people, and also the French, have been noted as the most remarkable watch and clock makers of the world. Nancy is not very far from Switzerland and perhaps the knowledge which this boy has gained while building his Meccano clock will start him along a line of clock inventions and perfections which will some day make him the leading clock manufacturer of the world. This boy also won a share in the grand prize offered by Meccano for good models.

Another boy, who also lives in France, but in the big City of Paris, made a miniature sewing machine that sews just like the big one your mother has. He shared the second prize. An English boy built an automobile that would run along the floor, that had two different speeds, that had a reversing mechanism, that had headlights and a driver's seat, and a steering wheel and a tonneau, just like a real automobile. It ran with the Meccano spring motor, and he, too, shared the second prize. An American boy who lives in the big city of New York made the safe shown on this page. The door has a combination lock and the whole safe is made entirely with Meccano parts. It has little shelves and compartments inside just like the big safes you see in any bank. The combination lock on the door is so perfect that no one who doesn't know the combination can open the

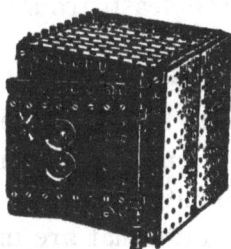

safe; yet this boy knows just how to turn the little knobs that work the combination and can open the same without the least trouble. Some day this boy might put into actual practice the principles he learned while making this safe, and he might even become the celebrated inventor of an entirely new kind of combination lock for the big safes and vaults that are used all over the country to keep burglars, thieves and robbers out of money vaults in trust companies and banks.

The English boy who invented and built the armored motor car on this page must have had his imagination inflamed by the stories of how real armored motor cars are used in battles. Perhaps his home in England is near the place where some of these armored motor cars are built and he has seen them

100

and built this one just like the real ones he saw. Perhaps as he was building this car, he was thinking what a wonderful thing it would be to run a real one and go to war and earn a great name for himself by heroic deeds. Perhaps as he built this car he was planning to be a British hero and die for his country, if need be, when he grew older.

In the last prize contest there were over ten thousand models submitted by boys—just think of how many different things can be made with Meccano. They came from the United States, from England, from France, from Canada, from Ireland and other countries. These models were of almost every kind of machine and structure. There were models of wire rope making machines, steam shovels, swinging boats, seaming machines, drilling machines, mangling machines, tool making machines, Zeppelin airships, grass cutters, deck chairs, jack-knife bridges, horizontal beam engines, road scrapers, letter scales, double acting wind-mill pumps, siege guns, automatic chocolate and gum vending machines, mowing machines, mechanical hammers, trip hammers, pile drivers, merry-go-rounds, giant see-saws, scenic railroads, roller coasters—a list of all of them would fill all the rest of the pages of this book. Printing presses, too, were built and submitted by some boys. The one in particular shown on this page is a perfect miniature model of a Gordon Printing Press. It was made by a boy in London, England.

But one model that almost every boy will be very much interested in is the one of an electric locomotive, shown on page 103, built by an American boy. This is a close duplicate of the enormous, powerful electric locomotives that are used by the great Pennsylvania Railroad to pull the fast express trains from the Pennsylvania Depot in New York City through the tunnel under the Hudson River and out into New Jersey, where the steam locomotives are hooked on to pull the great trains across the country. This Meccano electric locomotive runs on a regular track, with a third rail, and gets its power from three ordinary dry batteries which operate the Meccano electric motor built into the locomotive. This boy makes his electric locomotive whiz up and down the track, stop at stations and start again and switch over on to another track just like the big real ones do. He certainly must have a fine time with his Meccano toy; and when he gets tired of the electric locomotive, he can take it apart and build something else.

Can you not understand, now that you have read about and seen pictures of

some of the interesting things that can
be made with Meccano, what a very
great advantage the inter-change-ability
feature of all Meccano parts is? Do
you now see how easy it is for any boy
to build one thing, then take it apart
and build something else, then take that
apart and build still more things? This
inter-change-ability is one of the most
important features of Meccano. In fact,
it is so important that every part that
has ever been made to go with Meccano
outfits can be used with any other part
that has ever been made. And that principle of inter-change-ability is going to
be continued in all Meccano outfits.

So many boys who already own Meccano outfits have wanted to enlarge their
outfits and make them better and even
more useful, that Frank Hornby has perfected a Young Inventors' Accessory
Outfit which contains all the parts with
which any boy can build new and ad-
vanced models. Any boy who has a
Meccano set ought to have this In-

ventors' Accessory Outfit, because it contains many new parts that will make Meccano-cal Engineering much more fun — much more interesting — much more instructive.

CHAPTER IX.

FRANK HORNBY'S LATEST INVENTION.

Frank Hornby's latest invention is an electric motor. This motor is the most powerful and reliable for its size ever introduced in any country in the world.

It is not just an electric motor, built by an ordinary manufacturer. It is a Meccano Electric Motor.

It is interchangeable in that it can be adapted to almost any kind of working model. That is, when you are building a train, or a bridge, or an elevator, or a lift-bridge, or a draw-bridge, or an electric locomotive, or a Ferris wheel, or a tower or any other form of engineering in miniature, you will have an electric motor which can be made an integral part of your machinery. It has the Meccano equidistant holes (meaning the little round holes each one-half inch apart) for coupling it with the rest of your Meccano system. Furthermore, if it does not give as much power as you want, you can take the gear wheels and shaftings and even a worm gear and other parts of your Meccano outfit and build up gearing so as to make the motor as powerful in its leverage as you want it to be.

107

When the Meccano Electric Motor is correctly geared, as shown in the picture on this page, it will lift thirty pounds dead weight. It is also furnished with extra gears and has a starting, stopping and reversing lever.

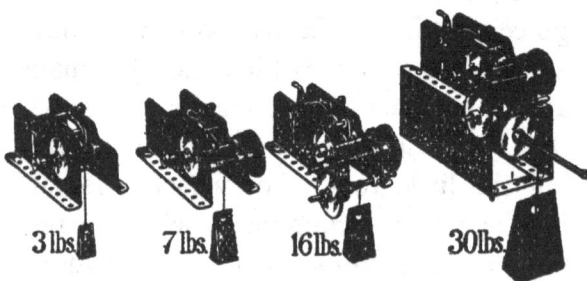

3 lbs.   7 lbs.   16 lbs.   30 lbs.

There never was a boy who did not like to see the wheels go round. Anything that moves is interesting. Any piece of machinery which just stands still after it is completed, is not nearly so interesting. You want your Meccano toys—your Meccano-cal engineering—to do actual work, to lift weights, to run the machinery. A crane must move, must lift things, must carry them around

108

and put them down. An incline plane car must run up and down as it takes coal out of a mine, or ascending the steep side of a mountain. A draw-bridge must lift or turn around, a Ferris wheel must revolve, an Eiffel tower must have an elevator running to the top and back.

And another thing, the practical boy is not satisfied to simply see the wheels go round. He wants his machinery—his Meccano-cal engineering — to really work, to really do something worth while; not just move.

Now with this marvelous little Meccano Electric Motor, everything can be made to move, to work. A derrick can be operated with it. The electric locomotive can be made to run along the track, with power supplied by batteries to the third rail. It can even be made to draw other cars along the track. An elevated railroad can be built and trains run along just like a real elevated rail-

road. A subway—you can really build one under the ground—with trains, trolley cars, a machine shop with drills, planes, die stamps and other machinery, can all be run by this powerful little motor. You can build a merry-go-round, scenic railway, roller coaster, and a Ferris wheel and make them run just like the real ones do at the circus or fair.

Every boy wants to be clean and strong and useful. The only reason he is bad, is because he is not busy with something in which he is interested. Meccano is not only a great educational force, but is a great moral power in making boys' characters strong, so that they will grow up to be useful, successful leaders of men. Meccano electrified is a remarkable character builder, because it keeps the boy interested, it teaches him and it amuses him.

CHAPTER X.

FRANK HORNBY'S MOTTO.

Frank Hornby's life has been devoted to helpfulness. He has, to be sure, made a million dollars or more with the Meccano toy which he invented. He is now a successful business man, known in many countries, and honored wherever he is known, but his spirit of helpfulness has permeated the whole business organization which manufactures and sells Meccano.

The Boy Scouts idea is to do a helpful deed every day. Meccano is built on the principle of helpfulness. That is on the true principle of self help. It gives every boy the opportunity to learn (while he is playing) how to do things that will help him to be successful when he becomes a man.

112

PACKING ROOM PRESENT FACTORY.

Samuel Smiles and all the other noted writers and celebrated inventors did a wonderful work when they inspired Frank Hornby to invent Meccano, and thereby put into all boys' hands all over the world a toy which they could play with day after day, year after year, and all the time grow more skillful in working out the problems which in after life, as they became men, they would have to work out for themselves or their employers.

Meccano teaches the correct principles of mechanics, and mechanical science. It shows a boy how bridges are built, how steel structural work is carried on, how automobiles run, how electric locomotives are operated, how wind-mills are built—it teaches him the fundamental principles of mechanical, electrical and structural science.

The boy who is Meccano-wise is the boy who knows these things. He is the boy who is looked up to by his pals. He is the boy who, as he walks along

113

the railroad track, can explain to the other boys just why the bridge over the creek is built the way it is; why the big girders that form the span are bolted together just the way they are. He is the boy who understands what the gang of men who are working like a swarm of busy bees on the big sky scraper in the city are doing. He knows the principles of structural work and when the other boys want to ask questions about why this is done so, and why something else is done in another way, then the Meccano-wise boy is the boy who can answer the questions, and because he knows, he becomes the leader.

You might name Meccano the "educational toy," but that is too big a word and does not sound interesting. You might nick-name it the "Self Help" toy, but even "Self Help" does not sound interesting, until you get big enough to understand the hardships and problems of life. However, every boy knows what helpfulness is, and the Boy Scouts

114

are learning to do one good, helpful deed every day. For that reason a boy cannot do a more helpful deed or anything more worthy of a good scout than to tell every boy he knows about Meccano and teach the other boys how interesting and helpful it is; how it instructs them; how they, too, can learn the principles of mechanical, electrical and structural mechanics for themselves. Every Meccano boy should be interested in helping every other boy get a Meccano outfit for himself.

The motto of Frank Hornby is the motto of Meccano—"Be Helpful, Build on Sound Principles; Do Everything the Right Way—then though you may have to wait, you will know that you are building for the future, and that you will deserve to succeed. Build right now, with Meccano, and Meccano will teach you how to build right in the future."

CHAPTER XI.

FRANK HORNBY AS AN EDUCATOR.

After Frank Hornby had made an international success of his Meccano business he became interested in working out a system of mechanical demonstration for schools and colleges.

A great demand had come for Meccano sets, for use in class rooms, to show or demonstrate just what a "Diagonal Tie" is, or a "Braced Tower," or a "Trestle," or a "Universal Crosshead," or a "Block and Tackle," and all the other mechanical principles which the student must learn before he can succeed.

So Frank Hornby prepared a book entitled "The Hornby System of Mechanical Demonstration." The following pages are a reprint and explanation from that book. It is printed here for the boy who wants to work hard with his Meccano and really learn the principles of mechanics. It will be especially valuable to the boy who wants to be an engineer, architect, manufacturer or high-salaried mechanic.

The advantage of Meccano in teaching the principles of mechanics is that a model can be built, studied and demonstrated, and then taken apart and the parts used to construct other models; also the boys who go to scientific schools, learn the principles of mechanics and of mechanical science by making their own models and in that way having a lot of fun and learning useful things at the same time. This is just exactly what any boy can do at home with Meccano. He can have no end of fun playing with Meccano and at the same time find out about the different ways that construction work, bridge building, machine operation and electrical work

117

are carried on by the big, real engineers.

First, he can make a Simple Roof Truss, like this one, and learn one of the first principles that an engineer is taught.

This is the increased strength that is secured by using a girder bent at right

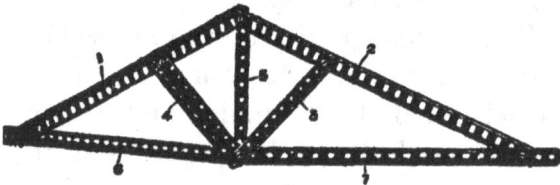

SIMPLE ROOF TRUSS

angles, as shown by numbers 1, 2, 3 and 4 in the picture. This girder has much more strength than the single strip because no matter which way the strain comes there is always an edge the opposite way which stands the strain without bending. The greater strength secured in this way is the reason you see these right-angle girders used in building large bridges, buildings, tanks and other steel constructional work.

118

This same principle is still further followed out in the Built-up Girder. This picture shows a simple type of built-up girder such as is used frequently in bridge construction.

The diagonal, or slanting part of this Built-up Girder and the top, horizontal

BUILT-UP GIRDER

part are constructed of right-angle strips, while the vertical supports and the lower horizontal part are constructed of flat strips. The upper boom of a girder like this is always in compression, meaning that there is always a strain on it, and therefore needs to be strong and rigid. The lower boom (2a) is in tension; meaning that it merely holds the other part in position; and therefore needs to be only a flat strip. This Built-up Girder is also used in

119

bridge building—you can see enormous big ones just like it in almost any bridge.

Isn't it perfectly wonderful when you think of the enormous big suspension bridges that span our great rivers; when you think of the great engineers who plan and construct these bridges; and then when you think that you can build just exactly the way these great engineers do?

But big and small structural work is not the only thing Meccano teaches boys. In fact, the boy who has a Meccano outfit to-day can repreduce in miniature practically any mechanical, electrical or structural machine or structure he has ever seen—or that he can imagine. In the mechanical or machinery line particularly, any boy can find a vast treasure of things to make.

You have surely been in a great machine shop where belts, and pulleys, and shafts were whirling around overhead. A picture of such a shop is shown in this book. In these machine shops,

120

where machines that can be driven forward and be reversed are used, open and crossed belt drives are used to run them. This picture shows how open and crossed belt drives work.

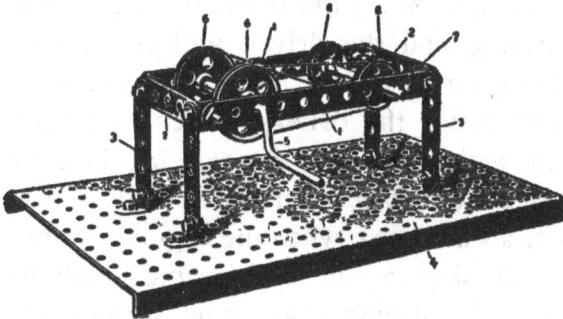

OPEN AND CROSSED BELT DRIVES

The crank shaft, which is the shaft with the handle (5), runs through the holes in the long strips, and the pulley wheels on this shaft are securely fastened to the shaft. The second shaft (7) is also run through the holes in the strip, but the pulleys on this shaft are loose, so that they will turn and the shaft will not. The nearest belt—and for belts, rubber bands are used—is an open drive, while the one further away is a crossed belt drive. By turning the crank, the wheels on that shaft turn both in the same direction, but the pulleys on the other shaft turn in opposite directions. With the open drive, both the driving and the driven pulleys turn in the same direction; but with the crossed belt drive, the driving pulley turns the opposite direction. So you see how in machine shops where belt driven machines are used, when the engineer wants a machine to run in the same direction that the driving shaft runs, he puts on an open drive, but when he wants the machine to run in the opposite direction, he puts on a cross belt drive.

If you have ever seen one of the old ferry boats that run back and forth across the rivers with its old style side paddle wheels and the big walking beam moving up and down, up and down, way up on the top of the boat, you must have often wondered how the engine that turns that big paddle wheel works.

Of course you know it is a steam engine. But do you know how a steam engine works?

Let me tell you how it works, and show you how you can build an engine like this with Meccano. The power as it comes directly from the engine produces only one kind of motion; a to-and-fro, back-and-forth or in-and-out motion. The steam is injected into the cylinder and when it rushes in, it forces the piston out. Each time the piston moves in and out of the cylinder, the steam is likewise rushing in and out, and so forcing the piston to do the same. Of course, the action of the piston is so rapid that you can hardly see it move in and out, but that is the way the steam engine is able to go so fast; that is why the locomotives of to-day are able to pull the big, long express trains across the country and travel 60 and 70 miles an hour.

But the paddle wheels on the steam-boat do not move in and out, they move round in a circle, or as the engineers call it, they have a rotary motion. Now, to change the to-and-fro motion of the steam engine into a rotary motion of the paddle wheels, a crank and connecting rod is used.

This picture shows the action of a crank and connecting rod of an engine. The guide strips (1 and 2) are the cylinder and the connecting rod is

CRANK AND CONNECTING ROD

3. An angle bracket is bolted to the end of the connecting rod at 4, and slides in and out between the guide strips. This angle bracket represents the piston.

124

This gives a to-and-fro motion to the angle bracket between the strips. The crank is 7. The connecting rod and crank are bolted together at 8 loosely so that when the piston is moved to-and-fro between the guide strips, the connecting rod will move in the same direction and the crank will take a rotary motion and move around in a circle, turning around on the bolt at No. 6. This simple model made of Meccano strips, shows the motion of the piston in the cylinder, and shows how the to-and-fro motion of the piston is changed by means of the connecting rod and crank into a rotary motion such as turns the paddle wheels of the ferry boats.

Now look at this picture of a model walking beam engine, and you will see how the to-and-fro motion of the steam engine is changed, and transmitted to the paddle wheel of the boat. The flat strip moves up and down in the small grooved eye pieces (4). This strip is in turn fastened to the horizontal strip (7).

This horizontal strip is like the big walking beam that you see moving up and down way up on top of the boat. At the other end of the walking beam is another strip (9) which is attached to the wheel (10). This wheel is fastened to the shaft that runs across the frame

WALKING
BEAM
ENGINE

and on the other end is the paddle wheel (12) that churns up the water and makes the boat go. This is the early form of the steam engine; one of the first types known as the single action engine.

Still another interesting part of an engine is the Centrifugal Governor,

126

which regulates the speed of the engine. The various wheels and strips in the picture are attached to a vertical or upright shaft.

A pulley wheel is attached to the bottom of the shaft (6). The top wheel (9) is securely bolted to the shaft while the lower wheel (14) is left loose. When

CENTRIFUGAL GOVERNOR

the crank (3) is turned, the belt will turn the entire shaft. As the crank is turned faster and faster, the wheel (14) will rise up on the shaft, spreading the weights (13) further apart, and putting

127

more strain on the engine, thus requiring greater power to turn it around. In a regular engine, when the lower wheel (14) has worked up the shaft a certain distance, it automatically operates a lever which shuts off the steam from the engine and so controls the speed without the engineer having to watch it. Isn't that a wonderful thing?

After the steam engine in the factory, or in the steamboat, or in the locomotive, or anywhere else that a steam engine may be used has produced its power and its power has been transferred from a to-and-fro motion into a rotary motion, it is then often necessary to control the power so that it can be used in several different ways. For instance, the power produced by a big engine might be entirely too strong or too fast, or too slow, for some of the little machines that are run by steam power. Then the engineer must transform his power, must reduce it or must increase it—in other words, he must control his power so that it can be used in any way that he wants to use it.

He does this with gear wheels, as well as with belts. This picture shows the usual type of gear train used in engineering where it is necessary to reduce

the velocity, or speed, of the power. The shaft (5) furnishes the power. That is, the power direct from the engine turns this shaft. But that shaft turns too fast. So the engineer uses a set of gear wheels to slow down the speed.

129

The fast moving shaft turns all the gear wheels that you see in this picture, until when the power reaches the shaft at the other end (2), it has been slowed down very considerably, and it is for use to run a machine that goes slower.

But this method of reducing speed is expensive because it requires so many gear wheels and of course, the more gear wheels there are, the more attention they must have, the more likely they are to get out of order, the more trouble they might cause.

So to overcome the inconvenience of the Gear Train, the Worm and Worm Wheel method is used instead in many places.

In this case, the shaft (2) is the one which brings the power from the engine. When this shaft turns around at a high speed the toothed wheel (4) moves around very slowly. In fact, the shaft must turn around fifty times before the wheel will turn around once. This is because the worm drive (3a) is

130

what is known as a single thread worm. There are fifty teeth in the large wheel (4) and as the worm wheel engages only one of these teeth at a time, this worm

wheel must turn around completely once before it engages a new tooth in the large wheel. Such an arrangement does the same work and fulfills the same principles as the complicated Gear Train, and it is a great advantage in engineering. It is often used to reduce the high speed at which an electric motor runs

131

so that the power can be used for operating machines which must run slower.

These are but a few of the wonderful things about engineering that any boy can learn with Meccano, and now, when you see what a very useful invention Meccano is, do you wonder that Frank Hornby has reason to feel proud of his invention and to feel, in the great praise which comes to him, well repaid for all the time, thought and effort which inventing this wonderful toy involved?

Meccano-cal engineering is such fine fun for boys, because the boys can build so many different things and because they build just like the big engineers do. Meccano is the original and only constructional toy that builds models that are true to mechanical and engineering principles. Meccano isn't just a toy, it is a real education in mechanics and engineering.

CHAPTER XII

AN AGE OF MECHANICS

This is an age of mechanics—an age of machinery. Many of the most successful men of to-day owe their success, and the vast fortunes they have accumulated, first, to their specialized knowledge of mechanics and, second, to the development of the particular branch of mechanics which they have followed. Thomas Edison is a mechanic, but in the electrical branch; Henry Ford is a mechanic, in the automobile branch; General George Goethals, the famous engineer who built the Panama Canal, while one of the greatest Construction Engineers this country has ever produced, is in a broader sense a mechanic.

The men who plan and construct the high buildings, the long steel bridges, the great steamships, the railroads, the subways, the airships and all the other great engineering projects are mechanics because their work requires a specialized knowledge of mechanics.

The greatest advances in scientific knowledge and achievement during the next generation are going to be made in the chemical, electrical and mechanical fields. The man who can invent a piece of machinery that will enable a factory to do more work in less time is hailed as a hero and rewarded accordingly. There is hardly anything that you can think of that isn't done by machinery. Wars are waged by machinery. The great guns are machines; the men who work them are mechanics. The men who make the guns are mechanics; so are the men who make the machines with which the guns are made.

Perhaps your mother runs her sewing machine by working the treadle with her feet. But they don't do that way in big factories where the most sewing machines are used. There they run them with motors. They might let the girl pedal her own machine when she sews the clothes, shirts, neckties and hats you wear, but it takes too much time—and time is money. Even bread is made by machinery now. They dump a barrel of flour and the other ingredients into one end of the machine, and loaves of bread, made and baked, come out the other end. And even there a machine takes them, wraps them up in paper and piles them in baskets ready to be distributed to the grocery stores.

Men in offices even do arithmetic by machinery. A mechanic has invented a machine that will add, subtract, divide and multiply and do it all quicker and surer than any man could do it. In the weaving mills where carpets and linens, lace curtains, cloth for your clothes and all kinds of things are woven, all of the work is done by machinery. One girl attends to several big weaving looms. If one thread on one of those looms breaks, the loom automatically stops un-

til this girl comes and ties the ends together again. She even ties the knot in
that thread with a machine—because she
can't tie it smooth enough with her fin-
gers.

Every man, every boy, needs a knowledge of mechanics. When you build a
wagon or a bob-sled or a roller coaster
or anything that you have a lot of fun
with, you are a mechanic. The man who
owns an automobile must know something about mechanics. So must the
man who owns a motor boat or even a
bicycle.

Schools everywhere are teaching practical things almost to the exclusion of
classical subjects. Boys and men are
hungry for practical knowledge. The
first consideration of the boy or young
man about to begin studying in a technical or trade school is, "What can I learn
to do that will earn the most money for
me? How can I gain a practical knowledge that will enable me to succeed in
that line?"

136

AN AGE OF MECHANICS

A mechanic is no longer considered a laborer. Even the men who put together the great bridges and the steel buildings, are mechanics; while the engineers who plan and superintend the construction are also mechanics.

Practical knowledge is every boy's fortune. No matter what you are going to be when you grow to be a man, a knowledge of the principles of mechanics will help make you more successful. If you are going to be a manufacturer, you will have to know the mechanical principles of the thing you manufacture and of the machines with which it is made. If you are going to be a business man you will have to know the principles of mechanics, because everything deals with mechanics in one way or another.

And a knowledge of mechanics and of mechanical principles is something which any boy can gain by playing with Meccano. Learning useful things with Meccano isn't like going to school and learning them or like learning them by reading dry books. Learning the principles of mechanics with Meccano is like playing. Any boy can have a heap of fun of the finest kind while he is playing with Meccano and he can learn unconsciously the things that will help him later on in life. He learns, but he doesn't realize it.

The greatest baseball players of today are the men who, as boys, started to play baseball almost as soon as they could walk. They kept on playing baseball until they became regular "grass-eaters." And in time ball playing became second nature to them, and they now play ball just as easily as you would run around the block. The greatest swimmers in the world are the Hawaiians because from babyhood up they live in the water.

Lots of boys remember the "Abernathy Kids," who rode on horseback from Oklahoma to New York City, and then rode in the big parade. They were the wonder of the parade. They sat up there on their horses with their little legs sticking out each side, and everybody who saw them wondered how two such "kids" could ride more than a thousand miles on horseback. But horseback riding is second nature to them because they had always rode horses and swung a herding whip, and cracked it like a gun. The most skillful and crafty guides in the woods are the Indians. An Indian can do things with a canoe that no white man could ever do. It is because Indians are brought up in a canoe. They spend the most of their time learning how to paddle one. The same with shooting with a rifle. The boy on a farm gets a rifle for Christmas when he is five years old. He plays with it—he uses it —until he becomes expert in shooting. When he goes out in the woods and sees a crow up in the top of a tree, he doesn't have to stand and take aim. He just puts the rifle up to his shoulder, squints along the barrel and "Bing"—the crow is dead. That's a lot of fun; but by doing that day after day the farm boy becomes an expert with the rifle.

The greatest skaters in the world are the Canadians. During the long winters in Canada everybody goes skating. Even the little boys have their pair of skates, and they soon become experts. They skate all winter, because skating is such fun; it is one of their greatest outdoor pleasures. They skate for fun, for pleasure, to have a good time. But while they are skating, they are learning. They are becoming more expert all the time. That is the reason why at hockey and at fancy and speed skating the Canadians can't be beaten.

It is just the same when you play with Meccano. You play with it because it is such fun; because there is such a fascination about building a crane or a dredger or a bridge or a locomotive or any of the other wonderful things you can make. You have a lot of fun, of course, but at the same time you are doing just what the Canadian boys do, and the Western boy does, or the farmer boy, or the Hawaiian boy; you are learning as you play.

The most expert men in any line of business are the men who, as boys, learned to do the things that earn them their living when they grow up. A knowledge of mechanics gained early in life will be an asset to any boy. The boy who gains such knowledge will find that mechanics become second nature to him, just as skating or shooting or swimming, or baseball playing, or horseback riding, or anything else that he does when he is a small boy. The old saying that "Practice makes perfect" is true. Practice does make perfect. And the best part of it all is that any boy can practice with Meccano and have a lot of fun while he is practicing, and can learn things that will count strongly in his favor and help him when he rubs against the real problems of later life.

141

www.ingramcontent.com/pod-product-compliance
Lightning Source LLC
Chambersburg PA
CBHW011204090426
42742CB00019B/3404